My Bug Box

by Pat Blanchard and Joanne Suhr
illustrated by Teri Sloat

Richard C. Owen Publishers, Inc.
Katonah, New York

I found a little cricket
on a twig one day.

2

I put it in my bug box,
and that's where it stayed.

I found a little ant
in the sand one day.

I put it in my bug box,
and that's where it stayed.

I found a little beetle
on a leaf one day.

I put it in my bug box,
and that's where it stayed.

I found a little toad
near the door one day.

I put it in my bug box,
and that's where it stayed.

9

It looked nice and snug.

Now where are my bugs?